HEARD ANIMAL

HEARD ANIMAL

VINCENT ZOMPA

DUSIE

Poems have appeared in the following publications:

Grateful acknowledgement is made to the editors and publishers of magazines, journals and chapbooks, in which pieces of this book first appeared: *Dusie, Turntable and Blue Light. Octopus Magazine* and the Apocalypse Anthology, published by Flying Guillotine Press (2011).

Cover photo: Vika Mno

Layout and design by DUSIE
Kingston, Rhode Island

First printing, Vincent Zompa 2014

All rights reserved. No part of this book may be reproduced without the publisher's written permission, except for brief quotations in reviews.

ISBN-13: 978-0-9819808-7-4

CONTENTS

I   A ROTATION OF HORNS   9

II   HEARD ANIMAL   37

III   TWO SUNS   49

IV   THE SEA OR THE CABLE   71

A ROTATION OF HORNS

THE RECIFE PLECTRUM

                        cuíca squealing   target burning
         creation spaceship one
                        when it arrives
      to converse with spirits
                        the mineral consensus
through thirteen centuries is founded
                    gelatinously spoken
    through each morsel tongue
                      right behind the spleen
     an if and when fragment
                  wherever there are five
    heart shaped boulders
                      thudding on the lawn
  it belongs to the eater
                of sunset water
a thrown into reeds baby
        washed up at that bend in the progression
where you've given up
                the last sluice
and you know you're going to
                have to enter the music
    to stop this drain

     let me in to address
    the thoughts on the leaves
        a red purling light
     you remember
   all of our spells
      our harmonic solar hexes
  two fuji apples
sit on the floor in translation
        focusing beams
    I imagine scythe cutting
through apple foam
  my heart word whirling
    cut and see look shoreline
and two have somehow
    met electric and pervious
      avoiding palatial hindsight
the mouse purple sleeve
    owl at twilight over the green held dunes
      and when he's dancing
  to the name of an unknown bird
  covered with strings
    her hair cloud is another bright spot
the sun itches in owl light
    slowly then
    each crustacean vibrates
      home the diptych

    astrolabe
                        begging angles
   or rust angels of telepaths
               in electrified clay
I swear your mouth
                     was meant for mine
then I thicken up the mountain
  too ganja   too concussion
             and the thirteen wings
     of the turbid animal
              or is it the blue insect
the tomb is dusty and buzzing
             under the yellow
      sheet thrust recife
               a phobia amen
    the last two years
    were a cirrus dial tone
and this unusual time signature
                 that's what you get
     for opening your mouth
        I was the director of haircuts
     or brutal eye gear
two sailors tilt of the earth
    or melville booby traps
             transactions
  that send black through belts
        and show
  the divine stitches on the human body
the hypnotist's walk away eye splits
             I would never know naught
  two way body splits

animal unknown to science
           implanted
              without haunches
    the trial a vivisection of hard work
                    and pluralistic bloodlines
         this is the thought   dear reader
            that the antiphonal note in colored ash
              is just a blip along the timeline
                         harbinger   death
    where I was greeted with an arching white Hello
                    and blue hammock sputters
           that quilt sonic uprisings
                each simulacrum looks
                        out the eyes of another wax figure
         hopeful but with a sewn mouth
                    say this   say that   say this
         and the quiet heartbeat you hear through plastic
                              is a metronome
falling through the pinkly painted quasars
                of a sorcerer spun universe
      that playground on the left side
              of the overgrown eyebrow of the caveman
       where I found a priests diary and drank it
                        the vibrating heart was spinning
         then foam dried along
      the lord's white dreadlocks and with the wine
it was wine the dead velvet
                         she said Horizon from the shower
         elaborate phrases on her eyelids
                  like ferns that through
            the window unfold

DEATH ROW CHEF
after Bern Porter

I dream
when the seasons change

      fluxed between myself
and the weather in my abdomen

and here the fusion of hysterical molecules
deciphers two souls

and horns collapse
up the same white frequency

Instead of stepping into the steet
          and knocking people's hats off

the blast is taken apart
so it can be seen in pieces

and each piece the flicker of an eye
reading one word to another

and each flit like a bird's neck
cannot slowly   cannot slowly reveal

the great cleaning product in rocks

In derby hats   in wheels
          on chairs   instead of chairs

of wigwam hats and the quiet people in there
around fires
        listening to the crush of asteroids
against each other and cracking toes

    and waiting on a porch for the host to return

and flat hills over imagined bones

and imagined bones
  forever cracking under the earth
        the red earth
and thoughts that can twist up
inside you like worms

and any good idea
  has certainly hurt someone far away

and he too imagined bones sifting up
    to us as the layers recede

through the great cleaning product in rocks

It is hard to leave even
  the things that despise you

for despite your attention
  the animal's grisly tusk
    can be used as a sword

 and every voice has an other
like the symmetry of two buttocks

 o yes
  like a rotation of horns
because our affiliations are sensitive
  because they are sometimes booby trapped

ABRAHAM LINCOLN PLAYGROUND

The wisdom —the smoke
licking out of the dark belly,

and seas whose markers slump —
It rejects and employs, suffering through
the turbid upturned graveyard.

Heaven sent apples.
We burned an old car in that part of town.
Luxury is more ornery I suppose.

Danny left through a gate in my hand,
falling in love with a stranger's cat.
I suppose getting rich is out, we said.

That man in the lightning might pull his face off
with a razor and slink back into white.

But that's fool's gold, the swift regal schist,
burrowing like an upturned candle
returning its name. Can I now die

so I can have a new moniker? Place weapons
of place in my hands. In fields, a grass blade,

in sofas, a cat on the remote control.
These are the hands, these are the people.

We agreed nighttime was out, and fornication.
A giant seabird perched on the world, a crimson throat.

That little ditty about the swimming vessel of our youth
was acceptable, as were table settings and lawn globes.
We would wear each other's clothes, but no others.
Ripening them with our juices and axioms.

He whose chorus would be his horse.
What would the neighbors say anyway

to our tousled hair. And maybe a frigate bird
ate my brainstem, who knows.

EVEL KNIEVEL

I am the white destroyer,
the hermaphrodite god,

scraping my feet
like a cat pulled out of a labyrinth,
then muzzled.

Lessons rise from the sand.
They possess the blue hearts,
then retreat back down the haloes.

Am I the man who gets mad
when people rub on me
what I've rubbed on them?

I am the replicated knife
worried how easy to slice the human butter.

My forest is a mask.
But this spinning pilot burns

revival candles until each graceless
blob on the horizon blows.

Stored in the old basement of the soup kitchen
or curving around the planet,

I am guided by the great beak
in the stars.

I do something
illegal to drum up excitement.

My love is an enemy.
My love is a boiling thing.

DREAMS OF SENSITIVE MEN

When that particular parameter of hell
broke loose, the piano collapsed.

I gathered the strings, the hammers.
Vanessa crawled out of the day, her lovely hips

aflame. Next door to her place
the drug dealers were always sizzling,

with cops throwing
their virgin eyes through peepholes.

I spoke with Vanessa before her oil ritual.
She had said she must often service the guru.

Hmm, I had said, but
she said we glisten without clothes, so I stayed.

These oils are natural, she said. They go
right through my skin and place the poisons.

They make the poisons mine. A buzzer went off
behind the wall every hour or two.

I knew Vanessa would perform her ritual
then smoke a big joint.

Her sister sat beside her. She couldn't remember
my name or which way to the sacred trail—

but she didn't know I was watching so much,
anticipating like a magic person,

of course, the testosterone in my mouth
delicious and sad.

In the kitchen I called uncle Walter,
my cousin in the East, and my brother in the desert,

for some reason trying to say goodbye.
I knew the obscurity— I couldn't

reach them that way. The stars were what
we talked about. To each I threaded a milky way

so they might at least think I was hurt
or strange, so they might have a sign

through which to recall a goodbye.
I hung up and slid back to the living room.

Vanessa had just aimed her five senses
at her spine. Then the lure,

the bone prism leaked,
and her servitude broke all over us.

PETER STUYVESANT'S LEG

I don't know where that word came from. I think
it's an old man's cane. Hangs above the door

like a thrust thing, its bodacious cells squeaking.
One lover rivets time to objects and closes

the raven's mouth to flurries.
One gets jealous of the animals

that are built to withstand weather, not to eat
all the other animals. I hang skein over Chinese

mirrors, trap mice in a skull with cheese,
then display my copper buttons in the parade.

I lift back the sash. Olya and Katia
are drinking wine and making love.

And shortly the dawn will come, each leg
hurting the same. Ten flagons in, the vale

of flowers bursts with souls of dead Indians,
alive again. I press talismans against the fort's gates

and nothing sticks, no imprints.

THAT AGAINST THE TERRITORY

I am slowly revealed,
empathetic and punched into this place

through the undressing code.
She is indeed dressed in ablutions and capable,

staring off into the woods
for a soul animal. She claws her way

back up the precipice.
The doorbell rings and it is her father,

a little dawn crazy,
his knives wet with weeping.

She is looking for someone to love.
My hands belong thirst and ribbon-torn,

slapped with wings.
I scatter my arms and hold a greasy

idea in the blood between
my shoulders. Her eyes say

ridiculous and she laughs.
One really has to have short stories

about the night's little paws,
she says, And sounds that don't go

too far, not a microphone
in the hedge, a weird pink light

on a telephone pole, or
Hey I feel this about your lips—
does it percolate?

GNOSIS

Persons are grey areas,
dolls blown through space over time.
Persons are waiting—persons to be,
persons to leave us.
They crank up new machines in the hay,
slip into something more comfortable
and exhume old planets
with high wire logic.
Persons, stained on the retina,
smooching each other's hands
when meeting
and liking what they see.
Ecstatic over firearms,
clams' polished hearts
and clean vistas—
persons, the gay sunflower of us!
How goes the person? It does not ripple
without forced entry.
The purple cadaver clangs
and another pops out, grunting.
Persons, the phase of jungle,
the nonchalant palace, sinking.
The bad hand on a good man.
Persons, quietly licking the universe, the jelly.
The poison arrow wafting in
towards the mirror's smile.
Persons paying bills,
waiting behind the kiss
and punching each other
in the mouth. Sweetly tackling
each other's torsos, vibrating
themselves out of existence.

CHUSHINGURA

I awoke after some other dirty business,
hung-over on tatami, at Kira's house
with a nasty bite in my shoulder.
It hadn't come from alligators.
I had dreamt of two snails
traversing two red and seamless earths,
like tomatoes spinning on their vines.
I knew if I didn't go now, I might never.
Kira's convertible licked the pavement hard
and spun out into the dawn.
The streets were wet with light.
My hand seemed to undress itself
as we zipped over the cloverleaf highway,
the hour after dawn, with no souls
on the roads clean bows. Let us go to the shogun,
he said. I remembered the night before.
His wife and friends, his stubble of finely ground tea,
the glass house on the Izu coast
near the run down alligator park.
Where are we going, I asked him,
his grey eyes still wet, red with whiskey.
The dawn was losing pink
on the right, up over the water.
You must taste it, he said.
My shoulder was burning.
We passed the sitting Buddha
and the white one whose head creeps
over the forest. We passed
where the Black Ships were first seen,
on a mountain a gondola creaked out to

over the water. Where a rusted cannon posed.
Where the land looked out.
Why doesn't it move, I asked him,
the sea or the cable leading out to the sea.
His eyes were closed. He said It is giving.
It is giving its slack. Soon enough the houses thickened.
Under the streets were other streets,
where we caught green lights until
the city appeared, dwarfing us in its cloth,
its rumpled morning of crows
fanning garbage piles. He said We are almost
there, pulling into the grey shitamachi,
the old town, what the Americans burned
from above, its shrunken streets from a time
when people were smaller,
where a white van plucked Mie from the street
as she walked home from the movies.
She remembered nothing after the hospital.
My throat is dry ice, my throat is raw egg,
she was saying. Kira stopped the car
and we stepped out. His eyes wandered like Borges
but he wasn't blind. I followed him
to a short red gate in a white wall. This is where,
he said. He looked at me, quiet. We stepped in.
I saw his eyes widen approaching the box well, the altar.
Nothing grew from between the flagstones.
I couldn't help looking. I knew he was certain
I had to kill him. The altar, the orange rind on it,
split into four leaves of a flower. We could smell it.
It smelled like violin resin, like a wild boar
hanging from an ash house's eaves,
like a head found in a slow inland river. Kira crouched
by the well. I couldn't feel my shoulder.
You can still see the blood on the walls
of the well, he said. He said, 1702. He said
Snow to quiet the feet. They dragged his deaf head.
They positioned the water.

THEN BURST ANOTHER

After all but the wild fruit
had rotted,
and all the people were gone
but the ones
who'd been out camping
or on missions to label the plants
and tag animals,
I culled the libraries of houses,
armed with a blue rocking eye,
and a segment
of what tree took my parents.
The idea was wearing a hole
through the ice I'd been consulting,
and for a while
it wasn't preaching
in a human vernacular—
the encoded waves of what spoke
through dead cars,
in wind that flowed
through empty skulls in the shade,
were still rhythms
I was taught at the local level,
telepathically, frozen in that end
of summer grammar
like a frog buried in a box
in my garden by an enemy.
Were it limpid in surface,
legible in the razor clam shells
I had placed on the shoulders

of poor Sonia's coat
like epaulettes she could someday
be remembered by, I could have seen
what was coming.
In my new library's section on Self-Help
and Mutation, I found the volume
that had been hunting me
while I'd dithered
like a reptile in the hills'
abstract abandoned houses,
the book on the softness of purpose
in organs, the book written
by one with the same name as mine,
with a picture of a now-dead horse
licking a child's hair on the front dust jacket.
And on the back—glamorous,
a studio shot of a man,
his shirt untucked,
an apple on his head,
his back facing the camera.

COTE D'AZUR

Careful what you say.
I keep my words moving,

ground between tooth and reframed question.
How many words at your access today—

are they like two lighthouses
calling to each other across the bay,

purling elongated to make sailboats tinkle
as they pass unseen?

And what malodorous danger
sets its sights on you,

whistling and puffing on two jetskis?
I dig a hole in the beach

until I reach inner water. Into it
I say Rules are meant to be broken,

and then bury that place like I'd bury
my favorite recipe.

I might forget its location
on the zillion grain star chart,

and that would be better:
I couldn't bring you back there.

ANATHEMA

Where are you blue cousin,
bomb of reverse perception?
Blubber of mine,
are you quivering in the meat?

You should be satisfied with your foot fetish,
sucking on the stones we have cut through.
You lick milk from the farmer's scarred breast,
musclehead. Guzzler in sleeping buildings,

in handbags, in eyewear, I will tear you apart.
I will tear everything apart, looking.
I will draw you as yellow birds in the marsh,
as a sick meal eaten as a rite of passage,

when every nine-hundred-ninety-nine years
you stick your head out the roof.
Are you adopted yet? Have you been
the stinking Amazon all this time? Machete,

let me see your hairy world.
How many feathers
on the creature you're wearing?
To rub in the river and froth in the fire.

Ramakrishna, code-breaker,
creepy fleck deep in the wood.
Come and get me.

LANGUE D'OC

In Marseilles,
Stuart Strange is burning in a minaret.

They set up microphones.
The sound of his body breaking
is the call to prayer.

Smoke riffles the sky like when
a new pope is born,
and heeled boots are back in most cities.

To make a good guard dog
feed any dog gunpowder.

In pets are enemies made.
The Saracens are fasting.

Why do they scream?
Because they are too quiet.

Stuart says, I'm in my own private bathrobe.
It's moist and warm in here.

He is studying at the window of God's house.
I'm in my little boy now, he says.

We read his lips through the glass.

The gulls circle and starve.
Tankers pull out of the mist
comme des mouches géantes,
like Artaud pulled from Rodez,

and high heels are now out.
If a battery is dying, bury it
in a houseplant for three days.
If the people are boring, start lying.

CONTAINERS

Yes, right now.

Right now there is
a snow owl somewhere close,
like a sexual odor.

Fingers at my temples, eyes shut,
I just know when something is amok
or around. I contain.

I never told you—
I was born with a tiny me
inside of me, near my hip.

Made of ox tongue and rhubarb.
Made of hair, bird bones,
a gas cap, some blueberries.

The surgeons cut him out
but couldn't resuscitate him.

They tapped his white lung.
They warmed him in ovens.

Afraid of what the loss would do,
they put him back inside of me.
Because of this, I can hear things.

I once hid
in the soupy light of a cow's stomach.
I lived on grass and a holy light.

I read my favorite book for years:
The Dark Book of Saddles and Brine.
It was two pages long.

Right now, in your brother's hands,
there is a lake wrestling its water.

How do I know? Believe me, I know.
By God, I am carried in two

like lovers in the blanched hand of Rodin.
Don't even fool around.

I met you in the blind neon chat-rooms
of a bridled and corpulent freedom.

On our first date, we licked
ice cream from the horse's mouth.

We drained children
from each other's hands.

We loved a night sky, and our necks
cracked at the stars.

I grease the forensic vibrator of forgetting;
it is large and electrically charged,
impossible to fit anywhere.

In the television
they are always finding things
inside of sharks.

Then everyone cheers.
A surfer's leg, a shopping list,
a license plate from an inland state.

What if they found my heart
in there, or a hot dog?

What if they found Mr. Olsen,
or his ancient purple BMW?

Or Siamese twins, like the ones
my great-aunt Kay was watching
one afternoon on Oprah.

I've never seen so many people
in one place, she said.

The two Debbies,
the two Vinnys.

HEARD ANIMAL

HEARD ANIMAL

I.

It had blown through faces,
swum in under the flattened cloud.

From the island it came wet and running,
reddened by the posing sea,

unnoticed in children's scrawl
along the dawn beach.

It was sand in our hair,
sea fleas pleading the position of science

along the ship's prow,
rusting half in,

half out of the changing water.
It nestled in the bobbing flash

of fishing vessels off shore.
On a radio made from an avocado

beneath the sun's clean splay
we heard it first

looping us towards
and away from shore.

II.

Nobody wants to stay in the noisy system,
ripped off
by a gluttonous doodad,

purchased
as any old thing tumbled from fog.

A hammock rocks in the wind
outside my thatched room.

The French woman next door
strikes a mesmerizing figure,

a flickering god
surfacing out of the evening.

Lantern on the beach,
who is your leper disciple?

      A single pelican
rings the distance between here,

the ocean-ground isthmus,
and the island,

sticking its porcupine shell
              out of fog.

      Night is lit up by Americans
pink daiquiris
and choruses of a khaki redemption song.

Some girls trip and go wild,
in margaritas the red lights hovering.

They lift up their wife-beaters,
unfurling mammalian milk flags

in the gaze
    of a third-world strip club jungle.

    The lights burn off.

Above, the French woman's freckles
revolve their pelagic home.

    Lord,
you are so deep
    in the jungle's wending scent

where a snow egret lands
    and is never seen again.

    I smoke in the outer palms.

I want to lie in the Mayan
waves with a promise.

Nobody wants to stay in the noisy system.

III.

From the jungle by the beach,

if the boys come at me
      through the coconut trees

holding the black sewer tube
                high from both ends

shouting Ay-Ay-Ay
      as if to take my face off,
I will stay calm.

I will duck at the last possible moment.

And they will veer into stars,
sandpipers circling their stunned crowns.

If they come at me with high trilling tongues,
          and try to roll it,

to take out my legs and leave me
      bereft of dignity,
    you can bet I will leap over it.

I am a poet for god's sake.
      My nipples flower silver at the slightest breeze.

I am cooler than the dead hand,
      held together like a sandcastle
    built by a Karate teacher.

On this beach I will eat my Torta Especial
    undisturbed and
        quietly darkening,

cooked by an equator, watching fishermen
        cast their tiny nets at a turquoise earth.

If they come at me
with the black sewage pipe from the jungle,

    I will scribble something brilliant
        without a single shudder.

It will be my last,
        most beautiful words:

    There is a man eating the waves.
        He is a bird.

IV.

If I didn't have this I would just be odd:
a lap dance on a flight to the Arctic circle.

Every eye is strange, thrusting in the trees.
How many hours it takes to land this flourish.

I might leave you, take the kids to Jalisco,
and come back singing La Vida Es,

La Vida Es only to find you're still here.
O Mexico. Damn you for you.

My precious cancer is the soul's
private role in religion.

I would love to say if I weren't here
you would make up my story—

worms live in someone's leg,
what the relatives thought was rice,

until they started paying attention
and the rice started moving. Like a god.

Everything says what you least expect it.
My mother says, Go ahead, smoke.

My friend Gaston thanks the Irish
for mashing potatoes. Holding your breath

under waves doesn't bring death but
a music more bouncy than any you've heard.

No scraggly notes oozing off.
Listen and learn. It is the sand crabs that position the sun

and its numerology. My favorite number is eyeball
found under leaves, almost stepped on,

corresponding to the Greek letter 4, which may be
how many sides each thing has, in thought.

V.

The cormorant dipped sea. Wind into shoal of sky.
Sand barks along the sea's perimeter,
stabbing the old giant goofball, thieving from edges.

I paint my own face on my fist.
It is a poem. I feed it sand,
hold it up and shake its head

at all the powerboats gassing up the gulf.
It coughs. It says a man should not write—
he should rove with animals in his eyes

but rarely speak of them or take them in hand
and say Dang, can you see this?
See the yellow under those wings? A speculum.

I can't explain. I make charts of storks,
where they land and how many,
which propels further charts on consumption

of vegetation in such abovesaid storkic areas.
I will leave through the wildest grasses
in your line of sight,

come back bearded and tell you of a kinder place.
You will bring your people there. They will
build on it. We will hate its guts.

VI.

    My word, Conch.
      If it were up to you
would we take risks?

    You spiral white
under thousands of years of blue weather
    and gold forecasts. Conch,
insistent and quiet, I still love you.

    You are who you are,
too old to be solvable by crowds.

How many cars drive down
your beach at night? How many slow

when they hit waves but keep going.
    Have we a record of such erasure?

      Gluglug.
    We keep track of other things:

    this is Conch, from Mexico.
      The record of what's missing
in the presence of what's here.

Coral is blasted out of the swimmers way
    where sea and sky meet,
and waves are their stitches.
        By rusting cannons,

    the bartender smokes and waits
        for a morning of French
    and Italian women, their fuchsia sarongs,
       flowers singing from
            behind their ears.

       Even so, it is still right
behind things, way out in the code,

where an array of doubles
    waits for word from you Conch,

to take over
      each mote's wobble
   through the straits of becoming,

each molecule's dark flit
          and bright stumble.

O this. This is just.
    Just this is. My word.

TWO SUNS

TWO SUNS

1.

You form the plucked language
of inquiry,

the of and of part of etcetera,
where the smell of two columns,

where imagined loves,
are fingers drawing scars in ash.

A conversation in a new language
with a beautiful deer,

like spinning under a dome,
forgetting your body's weight.

You said that I must first learn
how to love

and be good with the green lay of terms.

I had been chasing
the answer to the turning flame's tongue,

listening to O Bando Do Sol
when you spoke.

Because in order to hear it,
you said,

weaving nimbly
around the comings and goings of this world,

you must be lured to the verge
of death,

and some people don't make it back,

go too far out to that other place
of two suns,

one rising over this land,
and one flickering out over the other.

2.

I come at you nightly,
a cloaked and evident sprig.

When I try to sleep, I see
a black girl in a white suit

and a white girl on fire.

I will say anything for honey or love,
someone to recognize as I leave this world

where the raft sits for you too
through each scale-beating syntax,

a blur in a photo of the grand canyon.

In four hours I will reach out.
You may hide your face in my neck,

a thin cloth between the cut
and the harmony.

I'll leave with a wetland, its stock of mosquito,
anaconda, panther, piranha.

I will start pre-human so there are no mistakes.

Coffee-colored water, when the inner shields break,
do not blame me.

3.

That for all the look-away in his eye
the well-oiled path.

There are all kinds of gravies out there.

Of building up facts to create an argument,
of light spreading down from a scepter

of narco-stillness.

Like a repositioned rhythm on the beach
of her eye,

the radical nail poking out
of the unrecorded grove.

She wants him to beg her to come back,

having burst through the surrogate forms,

and if he lets himself go down that road
there's no waking up.

He keeps the zim-zaum mirror inside this room
to protect the other room from ghosts,

the room behind the wall
depending on the night voice.

4.

And even
those times are different morsels ahead

or thin segment light leaking out of the brown doorstep
parcel.

The thing I look for is more important
than the thing I look like.

In legs are the morals of upstanding.
I woke up in a windy arch.

Because I do not seethe down here,
even under the hot breath of short days.

What time did you send me to,
and what rocks are perplexed with green dominion.

I know all my footsteps bloom verdure.
The light in a can soils my feet.

It is twilight.

We are not allowed phone calls here under the covers,
she wrote,

though I do so appreciate you writing me.
In tropical germs, the spring of circumstance.

But here
opposing creatures might swim in, guys.

Through the lather, guys, the lather.

5.

Everyone rubs his feet together
before drifting off,

nerves like the decisions of anorexic saints.

Dandelion behind the ear
for protection from curses.

A smoke drifts in through the throat

on the night before the moon
flicks this southern hemisphere
with the catapult of winter.

In Argentina
defenestration occurs.

Outside the airport an ancient aviator
waits in bronze.

From the light eyes
we buy shampoo and sandals.

Everything's good? Yes, I am well.
There is flan in the silver fridge.

The children in the library,
the uncle in a speedo with a revolver.

Alone together for different reasons.

She loved the old stonecutter
down the road. A black dog,

a German Shepherd
bury coconuts on the full moon beach.

He wakes up one morning—the smell in her hair,
the morning skin on her neck smoldering.

6.

From each half of a maracujá
the sun drops upward.

Two yellow birds swing around the wood,

their bright skins not yet knowing
how to ask the question
their keening curves in from.

Tuned by hands that throw so much salt
as to be forgotten in wishes,

their –ness plucked like strings,
an other toothy sphere.

The sun drops upward
through blurred knowledge of death
and its environs.

Thirsting an invisible,
each memory spider flickers its web.

7.

The sun across the water, wet dogs clawing—
a formula to cloud the eyes.

The riffling sun
tattoos the sand's legs with surf.

We watch sun showers glimmer
from beneath a eucalyptus eave,

loving each coconut frond's lazy bend.
The enormous white fish,

its slow heart clipped with a blade glint
in a blue shack by the ferry.

Rain plows over
the elaborately carved human stations

cut bright green from the flora,
our carefree routines and heat slack.

The roads cancel out their destinations,
furrowed and bustling with mud.

To find a bone in the grass, the shells
let out a love-like gas,

and to enter us, the sky quivers.

8.

The jungle is a Portuguese helmet,
green-stitched with ayahuasca.

A whale's eye socket takes eight men
where the loggerheads build their nests.

At the leaf's tip
we feed the neighbor his own pig,

start giving away the Spanish neighbor's dogs.

Little moss grows on the side of the palm tree,
and the black dog buries coconuts in the beach.

The ocean covers them for him.

Agata knows a song about whales;
she is waiting for mermen.

Four years old,
she has seen a wolf eat a child in her travels.

Sticks poke from the sand
where the sea turtles have laid their eggs.

We love simply breathing, breathing,
and no one must convince us of anything.

9.

Hustling like a sidereal dog in the darkness,
I did not run into Stuart Strange in the jungle

but laughed barefoot and muddy
in my natural juice.

At every entrance,
questions of riders in blood colored boots.

She said I want a sandwich made out of you,
the way you collapse into my fur

and come out the other side
buzzing like an ancient telephone.

By the end of your life, an expert at boiling water.

Rib, sun, carapace,
an artful work being done.

Life is now real dirty, parents.

I knew my doom by his shallow grip;
it was like a distraction of clouds.

10.

                When I ask the dried
           but vibrating stalks of floating, half-human shapes

what feeds us through the styrofoam bits
                  and oil colored sand pleats,

        rice sits on the table,
              and whale bones slick with blackout

rise from the seaside dust like a monolith.
                  Ribs, giant skulls—

        it's all colored with love, I swear.
            Yet the humans misname the swaying body

        and throw threats over barbed wire
                  at the blur behind canyons.

        I know I saw different colored eagles
              down there, biting an inch of sky with each squawk.

        They won't let you damage my aesthetic
                  or call anyone over with special moves.

                The oil tanker bleeds black stars.
          Seagulls hang a blue cloth over a man
                like puja.

Let me hear you say Deepest Longing.

> The sand bugs reply, "It is all talking to you
> like the air through a maniac."

And the swimmers pull their new bodies from the waters
> like a lost gun.

> "Do not listen to leaves," they say,
> "little segments of dead love,

>> the pure songs of the past, where extinct tongues
>> radio in from measly dust."

11.

Eye splintered and ear whirring,
I pull into the old capital's dog light.

Matches are sold
on the beach's blank finger,

Tupinambá spills
from the rattling vessels,

and no hell-bent child
or man selling dresses on the afternoon sand

bores into the sandcastle's elaborate spokes
and turrets.

The molten portion
of some divine armor

sweats on a surfboard
out beyond the tankers.

Wherever they unbuild sciences
we will dip our organs to taste the sauce,

nights itchy with imagined hotel bugs,
while out the window our moonlit possessions.

12.

He had to buy a Mangalarga
for the drug lord,

landed in the trees

singing Lamento Na Selva,
fur on the underside of a leaf.

The capital burned, and he hid
from the bullets in the old hotel.

He could hear the wet boards sizzle.

Cesnas dropped in the green bushes.

On the third day out of Recife
a blind man in a white tent,
scared of his own blood.

He knows where in the chest to push
the needle,

the spell to bring someone back swinging,
a shadow in his tropical helmet.

13.

       I had forgotten about my life
for some time,

I realized,
       on one of those mornings in town

when people scurried through the rain,
awning to awning,

         as if hopping island to island.

    Then the sunlight hit the page;
the gorgon of my eyes
       in their personal steam

beckoned in ballads,
       in theological romance,

like bees in the grass
         around where we'd spilled a coke.

     I took action against magic,
against the burden of politeness,

and its scent of skulls drifting in
        through an open autumn.

14.

I cross
the red bridge to you,

say hello to the family
crushing red crabs into paste.

The cacao trees stand beside the red house
heavy with telephones.

The albino fishermen
pluck fruit from the trees.

Their boat flickers between existing
and not existing beneath them.

The horseman puts sunscreen on his friend
like a dark palaver.

I don't believe the soil
loves everyone equally yet, he says.

We leave for the island with a hole in it,
our thoughts the parted thighs.

I look for shells in the curling beach
and find nothing.

Drinking whiskey from a coconut,
we laugh through the island's mouth.

15.

Dog of my youth, run at the screen,
and say whatever comes to mind.

Is it true that a marker makes belonging?
The buoys, the ocean's slow undress.

Is it always night in the computer?
There are germs on the beach.

The dog was so timid, the letter deliverer
thought it might be her dead husband.

When you get old, shit happens.
Skin is a blurry lineament.

Most theater hinges on mistaken identity.

The hard plants still grow in the sand's
pluperfect mouth.

Teach your body
not to go down there.

Ice cream and driftwood,
the halves of a bee.

The blue skin that much slower each time
you wear it.

We can't believe you're alone here,
Horseshoe crab on the Oregon Trail.

One cloud passes under the other.

16.

I see every bone in your body,
plumb wetlands in my Salvador vest.

Our ancestors starving since last October.

The thirst for percussion can trade phalluses
and peek out of the moon landing.

We watch horses at the pyre.

I bury my hands in a glass of water,
then fold you into my smile.

People work long hours
and flood the web with promiscuous activity.

The adult world is the child's world,
just flat and gassy, father.

Lacking any elegant way to end it,

the good old boys wave to each other
over Spirit Economy Lake.

Lagoa Azul is a puddle in the grass.

We fall out of brown bread, mixing cows
and their butter.

THE SEA OR THE CABLE

PARHELION

There's a leap of knowledge in that cist,
a wink of tampering in the seven granules.

Hair in notebook,
cotton balls, the tombs behind nests.

I walk out of the sound of the cure horn
through fuzz at radio boundaries
where rules and local animals change.

I haven't seen your head by mine in weeks,
withdrawn into Etruscan.

Sign of the cuttlefish handshake, I belong

to the tiny filaments in your arms and legs,
the sweat cord flotilla of your neck.

I never know how to cure you,
kept outside the insects' hum.

They drain your face, they even out your dreams.

Someone brought them to us and said,
The human ear is water, its shouts still frozen in ice.

That human is shown an unending pasture to buy.
He says No,   I can't buy it.

    There is business being done here.

A MOTHERFAST CLOUD

Let us make everything right. Did you know
Slippery Easel or Marked Man?

Did your life vest cross a little sea
without you, nibbling on sharks?

The underwater misses his grandmother.
A wood floor, a mud house; there are tinder

sticks in the their lines. My brother
rolled up in a ball around honey.

Crying is the heart's way of stabbing: Please,
let everything be a little wet.

The hands are for covering.
Eight blooms wait inside the finger lakes.

You can't wrap a lake in a finger
or wedding band, I tell my wife, the Scythian.

Let us simply thirst, like starlings
with open mouths

unmoving on the dull cathedral lawn.
Put a sock in it birds.

I found a noise under them.
I put my fingers in their mouths.

MOONRAKER

Where I wake, blue and ungainly,
a hair pulled long in the wrong places.
The roof sings, a child in ice.

Where the bell spire prays.
Growing with a plant's dim grace,
an entire life a series of slurred moments.
Where we tire on thrope swing, catch

a Japanese couple's eyes, get burned
by other expectations. I think of other places
to go to the day before, when you waited

among the quiet pink lakes at twilight,
and Mercury pulsed in the underglow,
hidden between two shadow moons.

I bought you the buzzing slippers.
I was the one leaving notes around the house:

Bird petulant, bird acrobat,
upon the toilet paper's last sheet
a script written in prison.
On the whale you watched decompose

I wrote, Da coisa impenetrável –
thank you for the blue shirt.
It glowed like a skin in the gloaming.

THE STEM-WORK IS PREPARED

And then the skin phone rang

        and then the skin phone coaxed
        to me or through me

Of wafting of solitude of sorrow

    of saying

I pick up a stick and turn
it into a telephone

      In long creaking pastures
late night smoke is the next day's clouds

Then tiny yellow flowers
      glint in the cigarette grass

By the time we all surfaced the situation had changed

      storms of amber through
      the corner of your stare

And then the skin phone rang
      and then the skin phone coaxed

My dazed goat and his orb
the white lights on the hill dissipate

Of wafting   of solitude
       of sorrow

of saying

         (The desert has eaten so many bones)

SOLARIS

How do things drift away?
Dribbling pearls from the other corridor,
receptors hold up the tonic sunset,

calling down worlds off the palisades.
Who ever heard what she was trying to say
interpreted it wrong,

slapping birds against the vessel.
Sniffling on the fire escape, sliding
with a walking stick over ice,

she brings the beautiful bloodshot
out in this picture. One child
hunting with a knife and fork,

one child brazenly eating our leg.
For five minutes there will be no gravity
while the station adjusts.

Describe the ocean.
It gathers like molasses,
letter caught in my teeth.

Psychology regards the body,
sex regards the brain.
Keep this door close.

THE SEA OR THE CABLE

Here I am, mitosis:
the dirty hill and the white river.

Blue sanitarium flames   fall out the bottom,
and I'm smiling—dust, butter dish,

drain sludge that won't stop gurgling.
I gurgle back at it.
A hand in a circle is a tourniquet.

There is no more time for solvents, you say,
The coast is salt.

Stepped out of the wall
but couldn't drop yourself.

A hand in a circle is a spyglass.
A hand in a circle is a trumpet.

The dogs lather up the vest.
That day's sun in afterglow by Hell Gate Bridge.

That glare, I say, riven and rayless.
An Other Man was actually the title before this.

A Dog's Lung was the real title.
No More Kindness was actually the title.

ANTIOQUIA

I kept walking and two pelicans in the dark tree
   cleaned themselves,

    waited over the filthy waters.
         I saw a canopy with blue and yellow flags
              like a circus.

     There soccer players in the dust, a chestnut horse.

No one knew my new name, third vowel a target.
     I kept walking.

   I thought of her sleep on that other continent,
        a cat wintering silently, her white
nightgown, her miniature bridges.

     I met the pickpocket in Plaza Botero.

He said Once you have entered my life
     I can never forget you. I will destroy you
in memorizing you.   In green camouflage

    he touched me

   with open sores, with scars across Plaza Botero.
I said Every time I get on a plane I never return.

    The pigeons all rose as I tried to flee, but
        he shadowed my every step.

He said There is nowhere you sleep,
   you sleep everywhere.

AUGUST 20, 2010

Cannibalism is return to sender,
scorched and screeching at the holiday edge.

It graphs lies, refuses maps,
tries to eat all your words.

Cannibalism is the heart's way of saying
Sorry we're not hungry.

It does not touch the quivering beside you
and think this is skin.

Cannibalism is nihilism's crazy older brother.

It graphs lies, drinks poems,
tries to eat worlds.

It says go see the cathedrals, speaks
of wind in the foothills of the Andes.

Cannibalism slept on our eye,
crawled into a child's hand.

It washes your feet,
cannibalism bathes the graying face with sweat.

It lists our robotics on the soft back
of a calf's ear.

Cannibalism eats your laugh.
It is no more emotional alchemy.

It stretches drums overnight
on the wounds of the washerwomen,

leaves wolves in your lover's hair.

HIMALAYAN MUSK DEER

Where the network hunts, protect,
limitless air-plunged products halt in a cedary dusk.

This coterie of love objects,
their fecund stares,

their acrobatics forgotten
into the love-molecular imposter of dignity.

We show the house our tough frames and talk hurly-burly.
It is slow walking around the sun's hurled head,

our voices licking rooftops off,
piquant and kicking an invisible border:

that thirst of mind at you, that booty-shake
walking around the noonday with crossed eyes.

JUST A MINUTE, NOMAD

Hey, lay the burden down together, they said,
      so we told each other versions of the story

where each had to go to prison for life,
and it was our last day together.

I bought three white roses,
three red roses.

      I hoped you'd finally understand,
and we'd reverse the obscenity
we were taking part in,

          sullen and golden,

floating in the spray of each other's vitriol.
The poem about your hair beside me

      on the new white,

like strings I wanted to play
but hadn't been trained on that.

I trained only in dreams,
the blind currency of plant life,

finding weird blooms by the roadside,

the temptations of amanita,
      and the slow black minute hand.

I trained only in the skin's folds,
sometimes living only at night,

or lying in bed in the morning,
watching the blue sky

as the airplanes float by far away
every few minutes.

BEST LEFT RETRIEVED

Every time Não Identificado plays

I write the poem to your voice
        and our legs and our songs

Every time the slow yellow train slips by
I say   I don't need to be anywhere

       and I place two little ferns
            on your eyelids

I know each of your plants is a temple
to other lives

     The epiphytes hang by the mirror

       Upstairs the pianist rehearses
his suffering green dirge

I love to play you strange songs I hear
because I know you love strange songs

     the dueling computer birds of Tayrona

  the mules who bite the earth
and chew all night around me

    And the sea's whipped weeds
        write in our language of knots
about another place
    where deer tread the beach silence

  at dawn and they swing their wet eyes
toward you and you dream

LAND THAT SERVES THE HEAD

Sometimes it takes portent behind the voice,
one he should have recognized,

but fell in love with that otherworldly light
green and pulsing in the night.

Fell in thrall of stories
of the sea, its albatross stench,

                a black moon in black ice.

And trapped within the arms outstretched,
her round, excited voice and hangover eyes,

toes puzzled in moss and vapor,
the canyon mouth stretched out the vowels:

Terminus. Crosses were ladders,
chairs pummeled in doorways.

The lesser-known skills rub off into this dark,
no eyes or ears left to flag a car,

to position a rhyme in the moonbeam
or wear a magic man's shirt through his shirt.

Today is light for the first time in weeks,
brown water, glimpses of signs.

Someone says Psychology of the selves,
walking down Broadway.

And the lights drain.
And the rope evaporates from the flexing neighborhood.
Blind child, monocle, face.

HECTOR HYPPOLITE

Running into town for a buzz
they call me The Spectrum

though I wear no wire
under any of my orbs.

How grass turns into moonlight and then
shreds of sun fluffing down to greet us.

Hello, new season. Hello to you, sermon.
I awoke with a wilderness bite, the first warm morning.

Toiling in Sagittarius light, Mathania gazed
like a freighter to the rooftop.

I leaned back in the steamer chair until the roof
gave way. Then I was on the phone in the sedan.

Then I was whistling under Toussaint Bridge
listening for love echoes. Jean told me

about one world under the sea and one world
beneath the land. Only one is hell, he said,

and his eyes split into laughter like charcuterie.

In the center of Port-au-Prince is a park.
It is hard to extract yourself from me.

VALVE LIGHT

I tell you of the days we lived
in a forest and ate moss from the trees,

the days we slept in a volcano
under the tied tongue of a giant.

It is assumed that
the cataleptic catalyst whispered to you
through that morning's fogged ultrasound.

There were flames in the outer corridor
crackling through a child's megaphone.

Don't know for sure, but it's love
that steps out of the pellet gun wound
into the apothecary of the world.

I pardon every hand
with a dash of cigarette smoke.

But science is just now fondling the heart,
that thing made up mostly of space.

We fill it up with wine.
We stomp each other's white shoes and say Baptism.

Then we're dancing,
thrilled by a stirring cadaver.

I tell you of the wandering eye in my bloodline.

You can sometimes see it in pictures,
drifting from its mooring.

I tell you of the days we lived
barefoot on the island

and built steam towers
to collect the high lava fruit.

WHEN YOU CLAP HEAR THE MOLECULES BREAK

The late afternoon fades in blue light,
a white line of plane.
Where is the poem, you ask.

Why it's right here, my dear,
behind your ear.
We dig the hard dust.

We play games with each other's mouths.
The radiator sings bees, and the mirrors
of this apartment connect with each other.

If you look in the Mexican one by the bed,
you can follow the others all the way
out the front door.

The light traveling that path
you don't pay attention to.
I watch you on it from the bedroom

like an animal hidden in a bush.
You tell me your uncles carried
small broken mirrors in their back pockets.

They said they were used
to connect to those on other stars.
One star was named Dust.

I HEARD THE ONE-ARMED WOMAN SING

Drummed in through the green hill,
the birds click in the blooming ends

of May trees. My heaving has wanted
this life, its storm-tousled face,

its roiling gestures charging blue-green
through pusillanimous amoeba lights

and shoved-away hands.
I haven't soared into table crumbs, poked wildly

at the fire's packed morsels. I was,
and I was myself thundering across Loch Death.

The sound pouring out of morning
had that lemon sting. For every

forgotten song the labels pounce.
There is fog on the promontory,

a chance the stab wound holds a kiss
to milk and drag out of a lamp's circle.

The corks linger and sway. The corpses
follow their own scent, say it's something new,

can you smell that: garlic knots,
roundabout, tussle of cat hair flung.

I am positioned on a wind. I position a wind.

STIRRING IN THE WRISTS

I say This is my companion
when introducing you to the leaves.
Lay down and test your chest.

Dear snowbank, dear pebbles laughing
in the sun, coughing up the son-of-a-bitch

education has been difficult. Tracing water
through the heart's literature, I make
the mind hurt so it slowly breaks my heart.

And to clean up this mess?
There among the leopards, a gritty flung leotard.

Because this is how I taste, everybody:
I put my tongue in and the sensors honk.

And from among the carols, the loose tooth
is now chirping. The heart is simply homesick,
learning the word for window.

That winter's frost the only purified society.
The thirteen breezes come up, then
I walk out of the giant pose.

Reach down your sleeve.
That's the sound of the dogs

wanting to know what's behind
the door you're knocking at.

ORBITAL DEBRIS

Stretching his arm out the brothel, waving goodbye,

he swings out of the mirror, gilded by a whetstone.

Talks about parachutes steady descent
          during the weeks spent on a deserted beach,

salt as a phrasebook.

Then the high hum of a plane,
then a cloth falling from the sky.

Disarmed by his own comfort with the intimate,
the viral wet intentions.

A small white fly, a leg growing,
an opal ring
        ringing suddenly,
a lake's submerged church.

If outward spiral patterns, if seed necklaces hang
from the doorknob.

Level assumptions at his skin color,
his eyes the color of water.

At the cop's brothel
he can hear the silicone breathing
fragments of hell.

IN THE NUCLEAR ZONE

I travel mostly on foot
to leaven the names of the dead

where a cavalcade of clouds take umbrage.
They delegate authority to the promontory's map.

Dawn, ribbon, and coyotes
are received through their hands.

Our thumbs are stuck with their moisture.
To catch gold they must travel

far past the island where such things
were once caught.

After a long journey cross country
where trees puff and buttes sizzle,

their clothes take on the grain scent,
sit and hide in the cold eye of a lake.

They bury our names right here
in the starling's repetition—

A held door and thank you (dust).

RAINMAN

Didn't we learn nothing?
I see outline of my skull in your jacket.
I am alarmed, I suppose.

The thunder drove over us,
its cone making memory slide.

And when someone starts losing a past
what filth came over us.

The storm, the shooting, the rainman,
the lattice pattern of new eggs crashing down
like a lake where there was none.

Rainman, armhair forest that lightning lashes,
silence forced out of an evening.

Of an evening, and the snowglobe we live,
carry around with us.

What's it like being a kid,
your hooves just recently sheared away,
hovering in the wind like a djinn?

Its all rootbeer, dolls, and claymation.
The forcefield declines to comment,

so went across the grate, a body.
And so it freezes what we call our brother.
Naked man is the ice that covers.

THAT METAMORPHIC DRIP

When Pius XII tried to exorcise Hitler from afar,
did their blood change shape?

The veins in our arms fill with
a soft alluvial light, the sand sound
of the clock,

and overhead planes warped as film on gelatin.
There waiting beneath our hands, the devouring,

the devouring cleanliness. It resounds,
it piles up around the candle.
And if the thing we loved most started up
in a new direction without us?

The wolverine was caught in the mirror.
We wish we could keep giving.

Pius XII tried to exorcise from afar.
There beneath our hands, the devouring.

It softens and hectors. Glibly pollutes
that lewd side of the dish
we poured the reckoning from.

We just weren't going to anymore.
There are parts of our bodies we'll never.

We make a little exorcism against it.

FLYING RIGHT FROM THE BURN BUTTON

A selva está respirando, I thought,
and I knew it was your message
in my dream. Then the host fell

from the wine's mouth, and glittering
shoes reflected our destinies.
Weren't we in fine, dainty shape,

but for the hovering trick.
You said Meus pecados são proibidos
then resided in a wetland.

Inside you I knew that where
the stories disappear, here I die,
making masks out of a tree's skin

like a runaway. I guzzled several bottles
of ghost juice on the way for courage.
It was pointless and belittling,

planning an architecture for lightning.
I received several dream letters
from you. Dear future dead man,

they all began, and I reached
for your voice, a moon in Loch Gowna.
Ever had to murder a man with the eagle

in Jardim de Infância? Each man
must crack the air before him.

Vincent Zompa grew up in Rhode Island. His poems have appeared in Octopus Magazine, Turntable and Blue Light, Margie and other publications. His chapbooks include *Jacket of the Straits* (New Michigan Press), *The Recife Plectrum* and *Moonraker* (Dusie). His poems have appeared in Apocalypse Anthology (Flying Guillotin Press) and Best New Poets 2006 (Samovar Press). He lives in New York City.

www.ingramcontent.com/pod-product-compliance
Lightning Source LLC
Chambersburg PA
CBHW032131090426
42743CB00007B/564